T0165357

Strangers
IN THE MIST

LESTAT ST. JAMES

Order this book online at www.trafford.com
or email orders@trafford.com

Most Trafford titles are also available at major online book retailers.

Printed in the United States of America.

ISBN: 978-1-4669-9040-1 (sc)
ISBN: 978-1-4669-9041-8 (e)

Trafford rev. 04/12/2013

   www.trafford.com

North America & international
toll-free: 1 888 232 4444 (USA & Canada)
phone: 250 383 6864 ◆ fax: 812 355 4082

This book is dedicated to
Herbert James, Joyce Marie James
and loving memories of Donna Rae Webb

The Lion

At last she walks
Beneath the starry skies
to been seen by ghosts
Of the past
Forever tormented by the
Darkness of death
To forever walk among the
mortals of Life
This tormented soul can
Never rest because of sins
of the past. thus why
This tormented soul walks
forever among the mortals

Outlaws on the Run

We were just kids when we
started our destiny in a world
going to hell
We became what we were meant
to be.
We never could go back to what
we were before it all began.
We had friends for cowards.
kept trying to turn us in for money
can't you see they were no good at all.
we were men in a world that needed
outlaws,

So we became outlaws on the run
I told you we would be famous.
Jesse can't you see we share the name
and the cause.
Jesse can't you see we are family.
our names will live on through the ages.
we'll never be forgotten.
cause we are outlaws on the run

3

The Return

Tempted and tryed
and buried alive
I'll return from
the dead to seek
my revenge on the
one's who put me here
so don't rest to heavy
cause I am coming for
you

When I find you I'll
feed you to the
hungry lions that haven't
feasted in a thousand
years. so don't rest to
heavily your judgement
has come.
When it is light out
you won't see me
when darkness hits I will
appear to seek my revenge
and send you to the deepest
depths of darkness.

Payed the Due's

It's raining outside
tonight. We got done
playing a sold out
crowd tonight
of the all the standing
ovations and cheers
we knew we never would
be forgotten.
We were great and they
knew it to.
We knew it couldn't
last forever.
But we'll live on forever
in the songs we sang
now I am sitting here
prowning my sorrows in
This bottle tonight
and the deals we chased
away we knew what we
were doing when the time
was right.

And we payed the due's
with the songs we sung
and gigs that we played
they'll forget the times we had
you guys are gone
now, it's down on my
knee's that I still remember
the time with this
bottle my only friend
and I know that the
music lives on
forever, there will
be no encore for us
Just the final bell for
this life. The due's have
all been paid. goodbye my
friends forever. I'll miss you.

To the best band that ever played on stage I will
never forget the times we shared. Thank you
for the memories they are dear to my heart.

Tortured Souls

We walk this earth
you see
Blinded by the things
that are and the things
that will be
For the price's that
came to be were payed
in blood.
The tortured souls never
get a rest even when
they are laid to rest.

We go from there to fro
our roads are paved with blood
when we look around you see
we see only darkness.
The judgemental peoples call us
freaks.
They call us devil children
as the day turns to night.
We are the tortured souls
that walk among you.
Fear not judgemental ones
the tortured souls are coming
for you

Tortured Souls II

Tempted and tried
here I stand on cold wintery
night.
With no place to lay
my head.
and no home to call
my own. still I walke
this Earth, broken and
torn apart. will they
never know what lies
deep inside

betrayed and thrown
aside like yesterdays news
the evil of this world
will some day fade just
like the day that leads
to darkness. thats where
I will find my solace in
the years to come.
fear not evil doers the
Tortured souls are coming for
you.

A Fathers Heart

How can it be that her
eyes were as blue as the
crystal sea.
And her touch was soft
as the clouds in the sky
her heart was as pure as the
love I have for her
How can it be that my
baby girl don't see me at
all.

A fathers heart knows
no limits
The angel that she is
holds her fathers heart
in her hands for all eternity
she was as tiny as the speckle
in my eye
she is as beautiful as the
stars in the sky
Her tiny frame is apart
of me always.
For I am blessed to have
a fathers heart.
she is a blessing from above

Forever Apart

As the night falls to the
ground
and as the tears fall like
rain
I wonder what went wrong
and wonder if you ever
loved me at all.
The lies and betrayal
were to much to take
back.

You begged me to stay
and I left anyway.
You begged me to stay
But I walked out the door
Never to return to the
arms that I thought loved me.
Now the years have past
and I think about the
day I walked out
your door.
I simply say to lady
that held my heart
that I love you always

Circle of Trust

Here I stand
on this lonely shore
wondering what might
have been
And as the day slowly
turns to night.
the heartache still rages
on.

I never thought that
blood family would
be so mean to their own
now here I am the outcast
of them all
now the time has come,
to simply walk away
the circle of trust forever
broken, never again to regain.
someday when we meet on that
distant shore.
I will simply say I love
you and walk away

Diamond in the Sun

How could it be
that her eyes glistened
like diamonds in the sun
she was beautiful as the
morning dew that falls to
the ground.
Her touch was as soft
as the mist in the sky
Her hair was as brown as the
night sky.
Her love for me was as
pure as a new born
baby

Her body was as wonderful
as diamonds in the sun
Its a treasure to behold
the beauty of this earth.
as day turns to night.
this diamond in the sun
lays beside me forever more
for as a lifetime will
allow I will hold her for
eternity.
knowing that this diamond in the
sun loves me forever more.

Laura's Song

Today your memory ran
across my mind
It seems only like yesterday
that you took your love
away.
as summer turns to fall
and we start the year
that year is the year I'll
never forget
We were so in love
until that fateful day
in October of 1993

I saw that flash as it
echoed in my mind
your life taking as I
held it in my hands
Dropping to my knees
as you lay dying in my
arms.
Never knowing why
I'll always love you
like a moth to flame.
it never flickering
for somehow you are still
here with me.

Whisper in the Wind

The leaves are falling
to the ground
as the dew that falls
to the ground on a cold
winters night
Her walk is like a whisper
in the wind as she
strollers by.
Her accent lifts me higher
and higher off the ground.
Her touch is as gentle as the
whisper in the wind

Her love is as pure as
the snow that falls in late
December.
It is the powers to be
that brought that angel
to me.
For god and god alone
has pre-arranged this meeting
in Heaven
For she is my whisper in
the wind.

A Lifetime of Love

It only seems like yesterday
when I first saw you smile
oh and what a beautiful smile it was
I fell in love with you from the start
I will never stop loving you and
our beautiful children.
I have never had anyone thats offered
me a lifetime of love
I am so grateful to you, for the love
you give me.

I promise to always be
at your side. To take care of you
and our lovely children.
having a baby with you will always
be my honor. Because I love you
with all my heart and soul.
I want to someday make you my wife
cause with us it will always be a
lifetime of love

The Truth

I never understood
a thing until I got
older
Why they feared me
Why they hated me
Why they gave me up
I knew they didn't love
me.
But I didn't give a damn
I am the lone wolf
on this lonely trial
But everyone saw the pain
in my eyes and the
tears in my heart

I was bad from the start
They knew it I knew it to
But forget—them I don't
need them
Let them burn in hell
I am the only passenger
on this ride tonight
no one can hide the truth
no matter who you are
I made out on my own
Just fine, my heart was always
black as stone. I don't need them
I am the only rider on this rollercoaster
called life.

Loving You

How can you walk away
from everything you know
when you love her so
How can you hold on to
the dream when she
keeps walking out the door
so tonight I'll sing this
song alone. Baby you
Don't have to go
But tonight I'll play the
fool for you.
When the smoke clears
I know that you'll be gone
again.

cause tonight this lullaby will
play. when the song ends
she'll be gone again
Her memory is what see's him
through and what he says to
himself as he crys himself to
sleep. I'm already loving you
to much. He see's her every morning
He holds her every night.
He kisses her lips before he says
good night, before the sun comes up.
when she comes to me
tonight, I'll hold on forever
I'll never let her go
cause I'm already loving
you to much

To the One I Love

Tonight was a hell of
a night
tonight u saw me fall
like a king from a
throne
and watched as they took
me away.
The tears in your eyes
tells the story of the
love u have for me
breaking ur heart was
not something I meant
to do.

sitting in a cold hard
jail cell made me realize
what I really have
and I love u so much
that words can't express
I am sorry I made u cry
I will spent the rest of my
days making it up to u.

In My Life

It seems like a thousand
years since I used to
walk alone
never knowing love
til she knocked on my
door that day a few months
ago
and said how she loved
me so
and how she wanted to
be my wife and have
a baby with me.
she helped me through
it all when everyone was
saying that I am no good
but the love we share
is eternal.

she is the most wonderful
person I know.
cause she takes the time
to love me so.
oh god how I adore her
so. she turned an angry man
into a loving man. They always say
that behind every man stands a great
woman.
she is the best woman for me
god bless her for put up
with me.
she has two beautiful children
that I adore.
and someday our life
will come full circle
when we say I do
before god and the world.
cause in my life now
I know only love.

Whiskey Lullaby

Tonight he sits at this
bar. The bottle
is his only friend
through tear stained eyes
he takes another drink
to chase away the pain
of the love he lost that night
He has to play tonight.
He tells crowd this is my
last song forever

They saw the pain in his eyes
they felt it from his heart
as he sang a whiskey lullaby
no one ever knew that night
that he had a loaded gun
in his belt
His final prayer was answered
when he sang a whiskey
lullaby

The Edge of Time

Here I stand
on the edge of time
with the comfort
as a friend
the lone wolf always
on the run
nowhere to run and
nowhere to hide
with a bounty on my
head
Here I stand on the
shore line of the passage
of time with no friend
the lone wolf walks alone
going from place to place
never finding a home.
Now time has passed
once again.

He never thought that
time was his friend
until true love knocked
on his door.
with the woman of his
dreams at his side forever
more the lone wolf no longer
walks alone, he no longer has to
to run and hide
no more bountys on his head
he can rest easy now in the arms
of the one he loves, this is the
edge of time.

In My Dreams

It seems like only yesterday
since you took your love
away
and at night I find
comfort in my dreams
when I lay my head
on the pillows that we
used to share, I am
all alone when the darkness
falls
In my dreams your always
there
There's words in our hearts
that we never got to say
so tonight darling in my
dreams lets say the words
we were meant to say
was I not what you were
looking for.

But in my dreams the tears
they fall like rain
and now darling we'll never
know what was meant to be
in my dreams you are always
there without you I am not
that strong to see it through
in my dreams I find the
strength to carry on
cause in my dreams you
are always there
yea yea yea you are
always there
In my dreams is where
you always are.

The Dawn Is Breaking

I've been up alnight
packing all your things
I put them in the hall
now I am crying into my
pillow
wondering what went wrong
neither one of us wanted
to say I am sorry
we let foolish pride get
in our way
we never backed down
we never said no
now it hurts to much
to let you go

I helped you put your things in your car
I saw the tears as they were
streaming down your face
from the fight we had
I know it was goodbye
from the start.
You know I still love you
so I'll leave the light
on if you ever want to
come back home to me
The dawn is breaking and
you still haven't called
so darling I'll be waiting
for you.

The Stranger in Me

I feel so alone in the darkness
of night when nobody cares
How I feel.
I have no friends when trouble
comes my way
will there every be sunlight.
Or will I keep these feeling locked
inside for eternity
will I lay here and say nothing
at all.
Or will I be so alone when
the darkness of night comes
my way. Or will I always
have the stranger in me

Blood Sucker

It been nine hundred
years of darkness since the
day I got bitten.
When the clock strikes midnight
I feed again.
You will never know when I
strike.
But rest assured on misty
moon lite night.
I'll be sucking the blood
from your neck.
It's been nine hundred years
of darkness. will it ever end.

Printed in the United States
By Bookmasters